Kids On Earth

A Children's Documentary Series Exploring Human Culture & The Natural World

Columbia

By Sensei Paul David

Copyright Information

Kid's On Earth, A Children's Documentary Series Exploring Human Culture & The Natural World: Columbia,
by Sensei Paul David,
Copyright © 2024.
All rights reserved.

978-1-77957-142-7 KoE_D2D_eBook_Columbia
978-1-77957-141-0 KoE_Ingram_PaperbackBook_Columbia
978-1-77957-140-3 KoE_Ingram_HardBackBook_Columbia
978-1-77957-139-7 KoE_Ingram_eBook_Columbia
978-1-77957-138-0 KoE_Amazon_PaperbackBook_Columbia
978-1-77957-137-3 KoE_Amazon_eBook_Columbia

This book is not authorized for free distribution copying.

www.senseipublishing.com

@senseipublishing
#senseipublishing

Get Our FREE Books Now!

kidsonearth.life

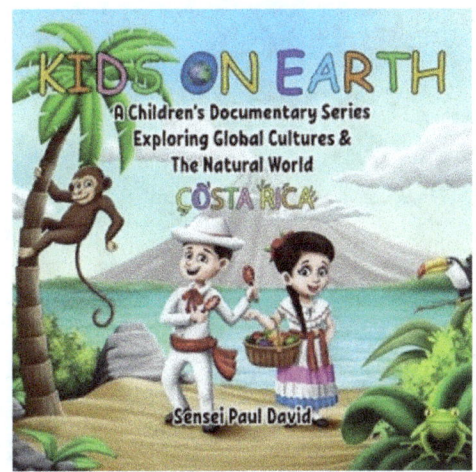

kidsonearth.world

Click Below for Another Book In Each Series

senseipublishing.com/KoE_SERIES

senseipublishing.com/KoE_Wildlife_SERIES

KoE En Español

senseipublishing.com/KoE_SERIES_SPANISH

www.senseipublishing.com

Join Our Publishing Journey!

If you would like to receive FUTURE FREE BOOKS and get to know us better, please click www.senseipublishing.com and join our newsletter by entering your email address in the pop-up box.

Follow/Like/Subscribe: Facebook, Instagram: @kidsonearth

Scan the QR Code with your phone or tablet to follow us on social media:

Like / Subscribe / Follow

Hello, adventurous readers! My name is Sofia, and this is my brother Mateo. We're so excited to take you on an amazing journey through our beautiful country, Colombia! Located in the heart of South America, Colombia is a land of rich history, stunning landscapes, and vibrant cultures.

Did you know that Colombia is the only country in South America with coastlines on both the Pacific Ocean and the Caribbean Sea? That means we have some of the most beautiful beaches in the world!

As we explore together, we'll discover lush rainforests, towering mountains, mysterious ancient ruins, and bustling cities full of life and color. Colombia is also famous for its delicious coffee, so we'll show you how our coffee is grown and made.

Get ready to learn, have fun, and make new friends in Colombia. Let's start our adventure!

FUN FACTS

Colombia is home to the legendary El Dorado legend. It's a story about a city of gold that fascinated explorers for centuries!

Hey there! I'm Sofia, and this is my brother, Mateo. Today, we're exploring the high-flying capital of Colombia, Bogotá. Can you believe it's one of the highest capital cities in the world, nestled at 2,640 meters in the Andes Mountains? Let's discover its wonders together!

Mateo: "Check out the Salt Cathedral, built entirely out of salt! Can you imagine building something so big using just salt? Let's pretend we're architects and think of what we could build with salt!"

Sofia: "And the Gold Museum here has the world's largest collection of pre-Hispanic gold artifacts. What if we were treasure hunters? What kind of treasure would you like to find?"

Mateo: "Bogotá is also famous for its vibrant street art and delicious Colombian dishes. Let's play a game: if you could paint a mural, what would it be about? And what Colombian dish would you love to try?"

Sofia: "We also love flying kites in the parks, especially during the Kite Festival in August. Why don't you draw your dream kite and share it with us?"

Can you find out what makes Bogotá's Ciclovía event so special? Ask a parent to help you search online, and let's share what we learn!

FUN FACTS

Bogotá's Ciclovía turns the city into a giant playground every Sunday, with people cycling, skating, and walking on car-free streets. It's a big, fun-filled party on wheels!

Today, we're off to Colombia's amazing Coffee Triangle. Imagine being surrounded by the sweet smell of fresh coffee – that's where we're headed!

The Coffee Triangle is a mix of three awesome places: Caldas, Quindío, and Risaralda. It's like a giant playground for coffee! The mountains and climate here are like a secret recipe for the world's best coffee. Let's go on a coffee farm adventure – you'll see coffee beans being picked and how they turn into the yummy coffee everyone loves.

Colombian coffee? It's famous for its yummy aroma and fruity taste. Here, coffee isn't just a drink; it's a reason to have festivals with cool music and dance. And yes, lots of coffee tasting too!

We've got a fun challenge for you: If you were to create your coffee festival, what fun activities would you include?

FUN FACTS

Did you know the Coffee Cultural Landscape of Colombia is so unique and beautiful that it's a UNESCO World Heritage site?

Next stop – Cartagena! It's like hopping into a time machine. This city has old stone walls and tales of pirates! Can you believe it was once guarded against pirates with big ships?

The Old Town is super cool. It's like stepping into a colorful storybook with its old streets and bright buildings. And guess what? You can taste yummy local snacks like arepas. Ever tried one?

Cartagena is not just about old stuff; it's buzzing with music and art. From groovy Colombian beats to awesome crafts, there's always something exciting. And when the sun goes down, the city turns into a giant party under the stars.

Imagine if these ancient walls could talk! What fun tales do you think they would tell us?

FUN FACTS

The walls of Cartagena were so strong that they'd been standing for hundreds of years, keeping pirates away!

Ready for an adventure? We're heading to the Amazon Rainforest in Colombia! This place is like a giant green treasure chest, filled with cool animals and plants that you won't find anywhere else.

In this jungle, you can spot amazing animals like the pink river dolphin and the sneaky jaguar. The trees here are like nature's skyscrapers, super tall and mighty. And the forest floor is a magical world, with giant plants like the huge water lily – its leaves are as big as a small boat!

The Amazon is super important – it's like the Earth's big, green lung, giving us lots of fresh air. It's a real-life superhero for our planet.

If you could chat with any animal in the Amazon, who would you pick and what would you ask?

FUN FACTS

The Amazon Rainforest is massive! It stretches over nine countries – that's like a whole continent of just forest!

Sofia: "Hey Mateo, did you know Colombia is super rich in plants because of its different climates? From rainforests to deserts, it's like a giant garden!"

Mateo: "Wow? What's special about its plants?"

Sofia: "Take orchids, for example. Colombia has over 4,000 types! Each one is unique, just like a fingerprint. And then there's the frailejón, a fuzzy plant that's like a superhero, capturing water from the air!"

Mateo: "Cool! And don't forget about the yummy stuff like coffee and cacao. They come from plants too!"

Can you find a plant in your house or garden and tell us what makes it special? How does it help our environment?

FUN FACTS

The Wax Palm, Colombia's national tree, is super tall, reaching up to 60 meters. That's as tall as a 20-story building!

Sofia: "Mateo, imagine climbing the Andes Mountains! They're not just mountains; they're home to ancient stories and modern lives."

Mateo: "Yeah, like a bridge between the past and now. People there grow food on terraces just like their ancestors did. And there are cool legends about ancient civilizations!"

Sofia: "And it's a playground for us! Hiking, mountain biking, exploring ruins... it's an endless adventure!"

What would you love to discover in the Andes?

Ancient ruins, mountain villages, or amazing wildlife?

Maybe even all three!

FUN FACTS

The Andes Mountains are the longest in the world, stretching along South America's west coast. That's like a giant backbone for the continent!

Sofia: "Guess what, Mateo? Colombia has beaches on two different oceans - the Pacific and the Caribbean!"

Mateo: "Wow, double the fun! I'd love to snorkel in the Caribbean, and see the clear water and coral reefs. Or maybe watch humpback whales on the Pacific side!"

Sofia: "Each beach has its own story. White sands, tropical sun, and dancing to coastal music. And the seafood is super fresh and tasty!"

If you were at a Colombian beach, what would you do?

Swim in the sea, build the biggest sandcastle, or go on a treasure hunt for seashells?

FUN FACTS

The Seaflower Biosphere Reserve in the San Andrés archipelago is a treasure trove of marine life. It's one of the most biodiverse areas in the ocean!

Sofia: "Hey Mateo, do you know what makes Colombia's government unique? It's like a big team that makes decisions for our country!"
Mateo: "Really? I thought politics was just for adults!"
Sofia: "Not at all! In Colombia, we have a president who helps lead the country, kind of like a captain of a soccer team. And just like in a game, there are rules, which are our laws."
Mateo: "Wow, so it's like a game where the goal is to make our country better?"
Sofia: "Exactly! And you know, kids can learn about politics too. It's important to know how our country works."
Hey there! Do you know who leads your country? Maybe you can ask your parents or do a fun internet search to find out. It's like being a detective discovering how your country is run!
Sofia: "And guess what, Mateo? In Colombia, people vote to choose their leaders. It's like choosing your favorite ice cream flavor but for our country!"
Mateo: "That's cool! I can't wait to vote when I grow up. I'd choose someone who loves nature and animals, just like me."
Sofia: "Me too! And did you know, that our capital city, Bogotá, once had a mayor who used to be a mathematician? Politics can be for anyone who wants to help make our country a great place."
Imagine you're the leader of your country for a day. What would you do? Draw a picture or write a story about your day as a leader. You can be as creative as you like!

FUN FACTS

Colombia's President is elected every four years, similar to many other countries.

Colombian cuisine is a delicious mix of flavors and traditions. Each region has its special dishes, but they all share one thing – a love for fresh and tasty ingredients. One of the most famous dishes is bandeja paisa, a hearty meal with beans, rice, pork, avocado, and more. It's a real feast!

Another favorite is arepas, corn cakes that can be filled or topped with cheese, meats, or eggs. They're perfect for breakfast or a snack. And let's not forget about Colombian fruits – lulo, guava, passion fruit, and many others that are both exotic and delicious.

Colombian food is not just about taste; it's about bringing people together. Meals are a time for family and friends to gather, share stories, and enjoy each other's company.

What's your favorite meal to share with family and friends?

Have you ever tried a dish from another country?

FUN FACTS

Colombia is one of the world's largest producers of coffee, but did you know it also exports more bananas than any other product?

Colombia is a country of festivals, each one a vibrant celebration of life, culture, and tradition. The Carnaval de Barranquilla is one of the most famous, a four-day festival full of music, dance, and colorful costumes. It's a time when the whole city comes alive with the spirit of fiesta.

Another unique celebration is the Flower Festival in Medellín, where the streets are filled with elaborate flower displays and parades. The festival honors the region's flower growers and showcases the incredible variety of flowers grown in Colombia.

These festivals are not just fun; they're a way to keep traditions alive and share them with the world. They're a time for people of all ages to come together and celebrate their heritage.

If you could create your festival, what would it celebrate?

What kind of music, food, and activities would you include?

FUN FACTS

> The Carnaval de Barranquilla has been declared a Masterpiece of the Oral and Intangible Heritage of Humanity by UNESCO.

carnaval de barranquilla

The Flower Festival in Medellín

Medellín, once known for its turbulent past, has transformed into a vibrant, innovative city. Nestled in a valley of the Andes, it's known as the 'City of Eternal Spring' for its pleasant climate all year round. The city is full of parks, museums, and modern buildings, showing its commitment to progress and culture.

One of the most remarkable things about Medellín is its metro system, including cable cars that connect the hillside neighborhoods to the city center. These cable cars offer stunning views of the city and have become a symbol of Medellín's innovation and inclusivity.

Medellín is also famous for its flower festival, a week-long celebration with parades, music, and, of course, flowers. The city's transformation is a testament to the resilience and spirit of its people.

If you could create your festival, what would it celebrate?

What kind of music, food, and activities would you include?

FUN FACTS

What do you think makes a city great? Is it the people, the culture, or maybe the history?

Sofia and Mateo are standing beside a vibrant, animated river, gazing at the colorful fishes swimming.

Sofia: "Look at these amazing fishes, Mateo! Did you know Colombia has some of the most diverse fish species in the world?"

Mateo: "Really? That's super cool! Can we find out more about them?"

Sofia: "Hey readers, let's play a game! Can you guess which fish can change its colors?"

Mateo: (pointing at a fish in the illustration) "I bet it's this one! What do you think, Sofia?"

Sofia nods with excitement.

Sofia: "Yes, and here's a fun fact: The Colombian Tetra fish can change color based on its mood! Isn't nature amazing?"

Mateo: "That's awesome! Hey, readers, why don't you and your parents search online to see what other animals can change color? It's like a treasure hunt!"

Sofia: "Now it's your turn to be creative! Draw your dream fish and give it a cool name. Maybe it can have magical powers too!"

FUN FACTS

Did you know the Amazon River, which partly flows through Colombia, is home to over 2,000 different species of fish? That's like a giant natural aquarium!

Sofia: "Guess what, Mateo? Colombia's history is like a treasure chest full of stories. Did you know about the Muisca people and their gold?"

Mateo: "Yeah! And I heard that the Spanish came looking for a city of gold. Imagine a city all shiny and golden!"

Sofia: "Look at these gold pieces! It's like holding history in your hands."

Mateo: (excitedly) "Let's pretend we're pirates in Cartagena, searching for hidden treasures!"

Sofia: (laughs) "History is like a big adventure, right? It tells us who we are."

What do you find most fascinating about history?

Ancient civilizations, explorers, or something else?

Maybe you can draw your favorite part of history!

FUN FACTS

Did you know the legend of El Dorado was inspired by a Muisca chief who covered himself in gold dust? Talk about a shiny outfit!

Mateo: "Hey Sofia, did you know that football is not just Colombia's favorite sport, but also a big part of our culture?"

Sofia: "Really? Teach me more, Mateo!"

Mateo: "In Colombia, football is more than a game; it brings communities together. It's all about teamwork, strategy, and having fun."

Sofia: "I bet it's exciting to watch a match in a stadium with all the cheering fans!"

Mateo: "Definitely! And guess what? Colombians are known for their passion and skill in the sport. It's a source of national pride!"

Sofia: "That's so cool! Learning this makes me want to play even more!"

Do you play a sport that brings your community together?

Tell us about it, and how it makes you feel!

FUN FACTS

Colombia has produced some of the world's best football players. The sport is a significant part of Colombian culture, fostering community spirit and national pride.

Sofia: "Mateo, have you ever wondered about the importance of mochilas in Colombian culture?"

Mateo: "Not really, Sofia. What's special about them?"

Sofia: "Mochilas are more than just storage bags. They're a symbol of our heritage. The Wayuu people, an indigenous group, are known for their intricate weaving."

Mateo: "Wow, I didn't know that! So, every mochila is unique?"

Sofia: "Exactly! Each pattern tells a story, and the colors represent different elements of Wayuu life and beliefs."

Mateo: "That's amazing! It makes me appreciate these mochilas even more."

Have you ever learned about an item in your culture that has a deeper meaning? Share with us what it is and its significance!

FUN FACTS

Wayuu mochilas are not just accessories; they're a form of artistic expression and cultural identity. Each mochila's design is unique, reflecting the weaver's story and the rich heritage of the Wayuu people.

Sofia: "Mateo, isn't it amazing that Colombia is one of the most biodiverse countries? Just look at these butterflies in the Amazon!"

Mateo: "And the Andes! It's like a whole different world. But we need to protect these places, right?"

Sofia: "Absolutely! Every bird, every butterfly, it's all part of our planet's puzzle. Like this Andean condor – it's endangered, but we can help save it!"

Mateo: "Yeah, even the pink river dolphin in the Amazon needs our help. It's up to us, and everyone, to care for our environment."

What actions can you take to help protect nature and wildlife where you live?

FUN FACTS

Did you know Colombia has over 60 national parks? Each one is a haven for different animals and plants!

Mateo: "Sofia, did you realize how many great scientists Colombia has? We're not just about football and music!"

Sofia: "I know! Like at this science museum, there are so many cool inventions and discoveries, all from Colombian minds!"

Mateo: "And look at this – our scientists are leaders in biodiversity research. They're protecting our unique ecosystems."

Sofia: "Education here really inspires creativity and innovation. It's exciting to think about what we can learn and discover."

What are you curious about? Science, technology, or something else entirely?

FUN FACTS

Colombia's Nobel Prize winner, Gabriel García Márquez, was famous for his storytelling, not science. But his magical realism has inspired many!

Mateo: "Hey, Sofia, guess what? I just learned that Colombia has more bird species than any other country! Isn't that awesome?"

Sofia: "Wow, that is cool! Did you see that huge bird over there? That's a capybara, the world's largest rodent!"

If you were an explorer here, which Colombian animal would you love to see first? Draw a picture or search online with a parent to find it!

FUN FACTS

Did you know the Colombian Andean condor is one of the largest birds in the world that can fly, with a wingspan of up to 3.2 meters?

Sofia: "We're canoeing down the Magdalena River! It's like a giant road connecting different parts of Colombia. Isn't that amazing, Mateo?"

Mateo: "Yes! And do you know the legend of El Dorado linked to the Guatavita Lake? It's so fascinating!"

What's a famous river or lake in your country?

Can you find a cool story about it? Share it with your family!

FUN FACTS

The Caño Cristales River is known as the 'River of Five Colors' because of the unique plant on its floor that turns its vibrant shades of red, blue, yellow, green, and black.

Mateo: "Check out the Cocora Valley, Sofia! These wax palms are huge, and they're Colombia's national tree!"

Sofia: "And the Sierra Nevada de Santa Marta is so special with its unique ecosystems. Did you know it's the world's highest coastal mountain range?"

What kind of landscapes do you have in your country?

Maybe you can draw them or describe them to a friend!

FUN FACTS

The Sierra Nevada de Santa Marta is not part of the Andes and has its unique ecosystems, including cloud forests and alpine tundra.

Sofia: "This Caribbean coast is beautiful, with turquoise waters and coral reefs perfect for snorkeling!"

Mateo: "And on the Pacific coast, we can see humpback whales! They travel thousands of kilometers to be here."

Imagine you're visiting a coastline anywhere in the world. What would you like to see or do there?

Draw or write about your dream coastal adventure!

FUN FACTS

> The Rosario and San Bernardo Corals National Natural Park, in the Caribbean Sea, is known for its stunning coral reefs and diverse marine life.

Colombia's handicrafts are a window into its rich cultural heritage. In the small town of Raquira, known for its pottery, visitors can see artisans shaping clay into beautiful pots and vases. Each piece is a blend of skill and tradition, often passed down through generations.

In the northern region, the Wayuu people weave colorful mochilas, each bag telling a story through its patterns. These crafts are not just items; they're expressions of Colombia's diverse cultures and histories.

Have you ever tried making something by hand, like pottery or weaving?

What did you create?

FUN FACTS

The 'sombrero vueltiao' is a traditional Colombian hat, recognized as a national symbol. It's made from a palm called 'caña flecha' and can take up to a month to weave.

Sofia: "Hey Mateo, look at these coffee plants! Did you know each coffee bean has its own story?"

Mateo: "Really? How so?"

As they walk through the verdant hills of Colombia's coffee region, Sofia and Mateo are on a mission to uncover the secrets of coffee. They meet farmers who show them the journey from seed to cup.

Farmer: "Here, try picking some coffee cherries. Feel how ripe they are!"

Mateo (excitedly): "Wow, they're so red and plump! I never knew this is how coffee starts."

Sofia: "And think about it, Mateo - every morning, people all over the world enjoy coffee without knowing this story!"

Do you drink coffee or have a favorite drink? Can you find out where it comes from? Maybe you can do a little research with a parent or friend. It's like a treasure hunt!

Mateo: "Hey, let's ask our new friends here more about how coffee shapes their community."

As Sofia and Mateo chat with the locals, they learn about the coffee culture's impact on the community - from economics to daily life.

Sofia: "It's not just a drink; it's a way of life here!"

Why don't we all draw a picture of our favorite drink and the story we think it tells? I'm drawing coffee, for sure!

FUN FACTS

Did you know? Colombia is the third-largest coffee producer globally, famous for its high-quality, smooth-flavored coffee. Just imagine the stories behind each cup!

Colombia's folklore is rich with myths and legends, reflecting the country's diverse cultures and history. The story of El Dorado, the legendary city of gold, has captivated people for centuries. Other tales, like those of La Llorona or El Mohan, are told to children as part of the cultural heritage.

These stories are not just entertainment; they teach values, history, and respect for the natural world. They are an integral part of Colombia's identity.

What's your favorite myth or legend?

What does it teach or represent?

FUN FACTS

The legend of El Dorado was inspired by the Muisca people's ritual, where the chief would cover himself in gold dust and dive into Lake Guatavita.

The Colombian Amazon is a vast, mysterious region, home to an incredible diversity of plants and animals. It's a place where nature still reigns supreme, with rivers winding through dense rainforests and indigenous communities living in harmony with their surroundings.

This region is crucial for the planet's health, producing oxygen and storing carbon. It's a reminder of the importance of preserving natural habitats for future generations.

If you could explore any wild place in the world, where would it be and why?

FUN FACTS

The Amazon Rainforest is so large that it represents over half of the planet's remaining rainforests.

Dance is a vital part of Colombian culture, with each region having its traditional dance. In the Andean region, the bambuco dance tells stories of love and courtship. On the Caribbean coast, cumbia and mapalé reflect African and Indigenous influences.

These dances are more than just steps and music; they're a celebration of life and a way to connect with one's roots. Festivals and family gatherings often feature these dances, bringing communities together.

Have you ever learned a traditional dance?

How did it feel to connect with that part of your culture?

FUN FACTS

The 'Salsa Caleña' style from Cali is known for its fast footwork and is considered one of the most challenging salsa styles to learn.

Colombia's geography is as diverse as its culture. From the snowy peaks of the Andes to the lush Amazon rainforest, the country boasts a range of natural landscapes. The Sierra Nevada de Santa Marta, an isolated mountain range near the Caribbean coast, is the world's highest coastal range and is sacred to the indigenous communities living there.

The country's unique position in South America also gives it a variety of climates and ecosystems. This diversity is not just beautiful; it's vital for the survival of countless plant and animal species. "Our country's geography teaches us the importance of respecting and protecting our environment," reflects Mateo during a school project.

What unique geographical features does your country or region have?

How do they shape the environment and culture?

FUN FACTS

Colombia is the only South American country with coastlines on both the Pacific Ocean and the Caribbean Sea, offering diverse marine ecosystems.

Sofia: "Hey there! Do you know what makes Colombia special? It's our sense of family and community. It's like a big, warm hug that never ends. Right, Mateo?"

Mateo: "Absolutely, Sofia! For us, family isn't just mom and dad or our siblings. It's our aunts, uncles, cousins, and even family friends who might as well be family!"

Sofia: "Exactly! And we're going to show you how we celebrate this amazing bond. First, we have this awesome tradition of cooking together. It's not just about food; it's about stories, laughter, and love. Want to join us in making some arepas? You can ask your mom or dad to help you out! It's super fun!"

Mateo: "And it's not just about our family at home. Our community is like an extension of our family. We have these cool local festivals and markets where everyone comes together. It's a blast!"

Sofia: "That's right! We dance, sing, and share stories. It's like a big party where everyone's invited. What about you? How does your family and community come together? Do you have special gatherings or traditions? Maybe you can start a new one!"

FUN FACTS

Did you know that in many Colombian towns, people meet up in the main square on weekends and holidays? It's a big social event where everyone dances, enjoys music, and just has a great time. It's our way of keeping our community strong and connected. Maybe you can have a mini-festival in your backyard with your family and friends!

Sofia: "We're at the end of our journey! Can you believe how much there is to know about Colombia?"

Mateo: "It's been so cool sharing our country with you. From our history to our nature, Colombia is full of surprises."

Sofia: "But don't be sad it's over! There's always more to explore and learn. And you can always visit us at www.kidsonearth.world for more adventures."

Mateo: "And remember, every day is a new chance to discover and appreciate the world around us. As we say in Colombia, '¡Es un gran día para estar vivo!'"

Keep exploring, keep learning, and who knows where we'll go next!

What have you learned?

Take this fun quiz to see how much you have remembered.

What is Colombia's national sport?
    A. Basketball
    B. Football (Soccer)
    C. Baseball
    D. Cycling

2. Which city is known as the 'Salsa Capital of the World'?
    A. Bogotá
    B. Medellín
    C. Cali
    D. Cartagena

3. What is the name of the traditional Colombian hat?
    A. Fedora
    B. Sombrero Vueltiao
    C. Panama Hat
    D. Cowboy Hat

4. What is a popular traditional Colombian dish?
   A. Sushi
   B. Pizza
   C. Bandeja Paisa
   D. Hamburger

5. Which river is known as the 'River of Five Colors'?
   A. Magdalena River
   B. Amazon River
   C. Orinoco River
   D. Caño Cristales

6. What is the main theme of the Colombian Flower Festival?
   A. Music
   B. Dance
   C. Flower Displays
   D. Food

7. What can you share with your friends that you have learned from this book?

Answers: 1B 2C 3B 4C 5D 6C

Thank you for reading this book!

If you found this book helpful, I would be grateful if you would **post an honest review on Amazon** so this book can reach other supportive readers like you!

All you need to do is digitally flip to the back and leave your review. Or visit amazon.com/author/senseipauldavid click the correct book cover and click on the blue link next to the yellow stars that say, "customer reviews."

As always…

It's a great day to be alive!

Share Our FREE eBooks Now!

kidsonearth.life

kidsonearth.world

Click Below for Another Book In Each Series

senseipublishing.com/KoE_SERIES

senseipublishing.com/KoE_Wildlife_SERIES

KoE En Español

senseipublishing.com/KoE_SERIES_SPANISH

www.senseipublishing.com

www.senseipublishing.com

@senseipublishing
#senseipublishing

Check out our **recommendations** for other books for adults & kids plus other great resources by visiting
www.senseipublishing.com/resources/

Join Our Publishing Journey!

If you would like to receive FREE BOOKS and special offers, please visit www.senseipublishing.com and join our newsletter by entering your email address in the pop-up box

Get Our FREE Books Today!

Click & Share the Links Below

FREE Kids Books

kidsonearth.world
kidsonearth.life

FREE BONUS!!!

Experience Over 25 FREE Engaging Guided Meditations!

Prized Skills & Practices for Adults & Kids. Help Restore Deep Sleep, Lower Stress, Improve Posture, Navigate Uncertainty & More.

Download the Free Insight Timer App and click the link below:

http://insig.ht/sensei_paul

About Sensei Publishing

Sensei Publishing commits itself to helping people of all ages transform into better versions of themselves by providing high-quality and research-based self-development books with an emphasis on mental health and guided meditations. Sensei Publishing offers well-written e-books, audiobooks, paperbacks and online courses that simplify complicated but practical topics in line with its mission to inspire people towards positive transformation.

It's a great day to be alive!

About the Author

I create simple & transformative eBooks & Guided Meditations for Adults & Children proven to help navigate uncertainty, solve niche problems & bring families closer together.

I'm a former finance project manager, private pilot, jiu-jitsu instructor, musician & former University of Toronto Fitness Trainer. I prefer a science-based approach to focus on these & other areas in my life to stay humble & hungry to evolve. I hope you enjoy my work and I'd love to hear your feedback.

- It's a great day to be alive!
Sensei Paul David

Scan & Follow/Like/Subscribe: Facebook, Instagram: @kidsonearth

Scan using your phone/iPad camera for Social Media

Visit us at www.senseipublishing.com and sign up for our newsletter to learn more about our exciting books and to experience our FREE Guided Meditations for Kids & Adults.

www.ingramcontent.com/pod-product-compliance
Lightning Source LLC
Chambersburg PA
CBHW080613100526
44585CB00035B/2403